Lifeboat Design and Development No.1

CLYDE
RESCUE CRUISERS

The RNLI's rescue cruisers, their design and history

Nicholas Leach
FOXGLOVE PUBLISHING

First published 2019
This edition 2024

Published by
Foxglove Publishing Ltd
Foxglove House, Shute Hill,
Lichfield WS13 8DB
United Kingdom
Tel 07940 905046

© Nicholas Leach 2024

The right of the Author to be
identified as the Author of
this work has been asserted in
accordance with the Copyrights,
Designs and Patents Act 1988.

All rights reserved. No part of
this book may be reprinted or
reproduced or utilised in any form
or by any electronic, mechanical
or other means, now known or
hereafter invented, including
photocopying and recording,
or in any information storage
or retrieval system, without
the permission in writing from
the Publishers. British Library
Cataloguing in Publication Data.

ISBN 9781909540156

Typesetting/layout by
Nicholas Leach/Foxglove
Publishing

LIFEBOAT BOOKS PUBLISHED BY FOXGLOVE PUBLISHING

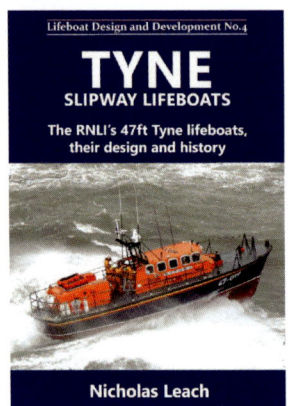

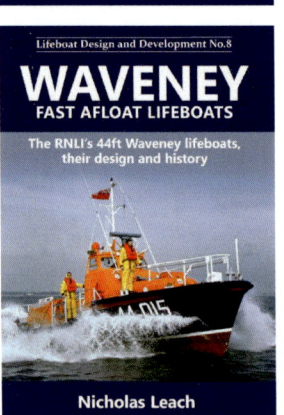

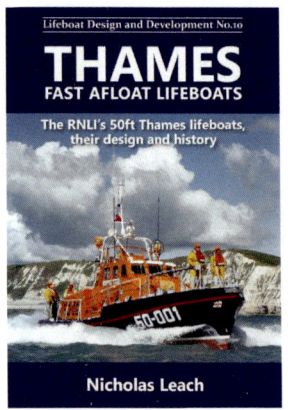

THESE BOOKS AND MORE ARE AVAILABLE ONLINE AT
FOXGLOVE-PUBLISHING.COMPANY.SITE

LIFEBOAT DESIGN AND DEVELOPMENT SERIES This is the first book in a series of concise illustrated volumes that trace the history and describe technical aspects of different RNLI lifeboat types. The books are as follows: No.2 Surf motor lifeboats; No.3 Atlantic inshore lifeboatsl No.4 47ft Tyne fast slipway lifeboats; No.5 60ft Barnetts; No.6 33ft Brede intermediate lifeboats; No.7 A class inshore lifeboats; No.8 Waveney fast afloat lifeboats; No.9 Steam lifeboats; and No.10 Thames fast afloat lifeboats.

THE AUTHOR Nicholas Leach has a long-standing interest in lifeboats and the lifeboat service. He has written many articles, books and papers on the subject, including a history of the origins of the lifeboat service; a comprehensive record of the RNLI's lifeboat stations in 1999, the organisation's 175th anniversary; RNLI Motor Lifeboats, a detailed history of the development of powered lifeboats; and numerous station histories, including ones covering the stations of Cromer, Longhope, Padstow, Sennen Cove, Weymouth, Whitby, Humber and Skegness. He has visited all of the lifeboat stations in the UK and Ireland, past and present, and is Editor of Ships Monthly, the international shipping magazine, and Lifeboats Past & Present, the magazine for lifeboat enthusiasts.

Contents

	Design and development	5
70-001	Charles H. Barrett (Civil Service No.35)	19
70-002	Grace Paterson Ritchie	33
70-003	City of Bristol	48
	Map	60

Acknowledgements

For assistance with this project, my thanks go to Tony Dixon, Tony Denton, Richie Leonard, Alasdair MacLean and Cliff Crone, who supplied photographs and information; Hayley Whiting of the RNLI Heritage Trust, who also answered various queries; Scott Snowling for supplying outstanding line drawings; Ian Moignard for proofing; Bernard Condon showed me over the superbly retsored 70-002; and Gerrit Malipaard, owner of 70-001, who took me out on his immaculate lifeboat from her home port of Maassluis, enabling me to appreciate the magnificent Clyde class rescue cruisers at first hand, and to sow the seeds for this volume. NL

Bibliography

Dixon, Tony (no date): Bristol Channel Gypsies (Edward Gaskell, publishers, Devon).

Fry, Eric (1975): Lifeboat Design and Development (David & Charles, London).

Leach, Nicholas (2005): RNLI Motor Lifeboats (Landmark Publishing Limited, Ashbourne Hall, Cokayne Avenue, Ashbourne).

Leach, Nicholas (2007): Orkney's Lifeboat Heritage (Tempus Publishing Ltd, Stroud, Glos).

Manson, Stephen M. (2002): Gracie, Mickie & Margaret (The Orcadian Limited, Kirkwall).

Design and development

The 70ft Clyde class, the largest rescue vessels ever built by the RNLI, was developed during the early 1960s after members of the Institution's Committee of Management visited the Netherlands and Germany, where cruising lifeboats were successfully employed. In particular, the German lifeboat society, the DGzRS, had introduced impressive rescue cruisers which were operated from key stations to cover large areas of the North and Baltic Seas, with the crews living on board. They carried daughter boats, kept in a cradle, which were launched through a door at the stern for rescues in shallow waters. Although the RNLI did not follow this model, after a review of this visit the Institution embraced the concept of a live-aboard rescue cruiser and in 1962 the decision was taken by the RNLI's Committee of Management to commission the building of two long-range lifeboats, larger than the 52ft Barnett, which were then the largest type in the RNLI fleet.

▼ The first 70ft Clyde Charles H. Barrett (Civil Service No.35). The Clydes were the largest rescue craft ever built by the RNLI. (By courtesy of the RNLI)

The principal requirements were for a boat of 70ft in length, with a speed of 11 to 12 knots. It was to have endurance suitable for prolonged search and/or stand-by operations and the capacity for approximately 120 survivors. The crew accommodation was to be sufficient for a full-time staff of five to live on board. The new design would also be equipped with a 20-knot inflatable boat similar to one of the then newly-developed inshore rescue boats (later inshore lifeboats).

Selected firms were invited to submit proposals for the design of the lifeboat, and a design was also prepared by the RNLI's staff under the direction of the Institution's Surveyor of Lifeboats, Richard A. Oakley, MBE. From the designs submitted, it was decided that two prepared by boatbuilders, along with that of the RNLI, should be tank tested to determine which hull form was most suitable. The other designs had been submitted by John Tyrrell, MRINA, of Arklow, Co Wicklow in Ireland, and the Herd & Mackenzie boatyard in Buckie.

THE FIRST RESCUE CRUISERS • The concept of the rescue cruiser was developed by the German Maritime Search and Rescue Service (Deutsche Gesellschaft zur Rettung Schiffbrüchiger, DGzRS), which introduced the first such vessel in the 1950s. Named Theodor Heuss, she entered service on the Frisian Island of Borkum in March 1957 to open a new chapter in the history of the country's sea rescue operations. She was 23.2m in length and was followed by three other vessels of the same size and design. They carried 6.5m daughter boats, and were capable of speeds in excess of 21 knots, with accommodation on board for a crew of four.

The concept of the rescue cruiser was developed in response to the unique conditions faced by the German lifeboat service. The boats face shallow seas near the coast, with extensive tidal sands, shelves and reefs, but often have to travel considerable distances to reach and follow the main shipping routes. Either numerous rescue stations with a wide variety of equipment could be operated, or a few large and fast lifeboats could be placed at strategic stations, being operated by well-trained full-time crews who would live on board. The rescue cruiser concept has been refined and developed since its conception, with larger and more advanced cruisers being built.

▲ The first 70ft Clyde Charles H. Barrett (Civil Service No.35) on trials shortly after being built. The boats were the largest ever built for the RNLI. (Beken, courtesy of the RNLI)

The tank testing was carried out by the Saunders-Roe Division of the Westland Aircraft Co Ltd (later the British Hovercraft Corporation) at Cowes, Isle of Wight, to assess the seaworthiness of the self-propelled models in different sea states. The tests indicated that both the RNLI's design and that submitted by Tyrrell had good characteristics and were approximately equal in their capabilities. The Committee of Management therefore decided to order two lifeboats, one based on the RNLI's hull form and the second on the Tyrrell design. Both boats had the same general on-board arrangements and specifications.

The order for the boats was placed with Yarrow & Co Ltd, well-known shipbuilders of Scotstoun, Glasgow in June 1964. The first was completed in August 1965 and the second in January 1966, and they were allocated operational numbers 70-001 (ON.987) and 70-002 (ON.988) respectively. The design was subsequently given the class name Clyde, after the river on which the first two boats were built, following the RNLI's policy of naming lifeboat classes after rivers.

CLYDE RESCUE CRUISERS

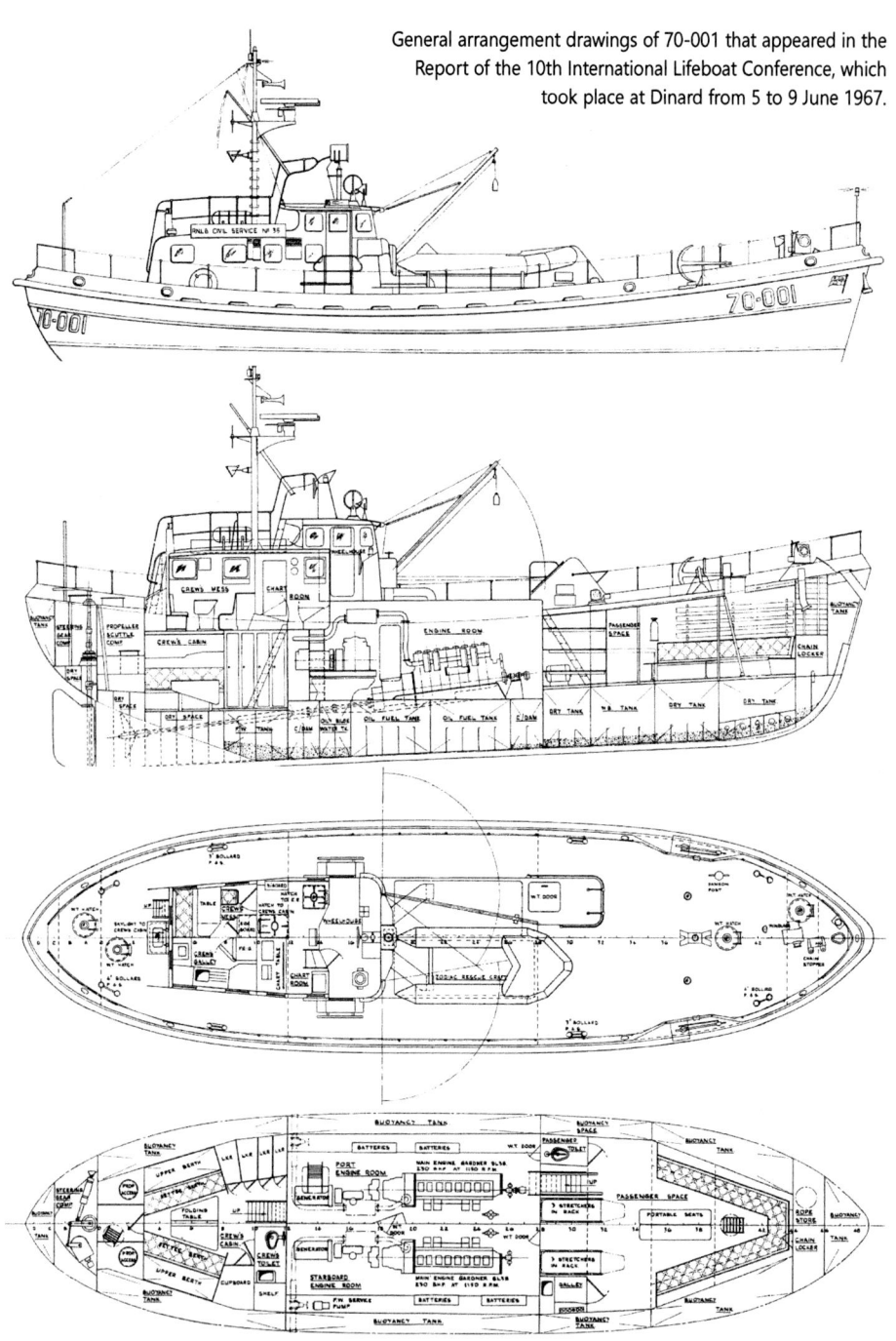

General arrangement drawings of 70-001 that appeared in the Report of the 10th International Lifeboat Conference, which took place at Dinard from 5 to 9 June 1967.

◀ 70-001 moored at Charles Hill's yard in Bristol Docks in the mid-1960s prior to being accepted into service. (Grahame Farr, by courtesy of the RNLI)

Although the steam lifeboats of the 1890s were steel-hulled, the Clyde was the first modern RNLI lifeboat to be built of steel. As the two boats were built to the same specification and general arrangement, although to slightly different hull lines plans, they were very similar in outward appearance, and the differences were limited to minor adjustments of the layout to suit the differing hull forms. Further alterations were made to the layout during annual surveys, particularly in the case of the survivors' cabin. Neither of the boats was self-righting.

Facilities were provided for the crew to live and sleep on board, their quarters being arranged below deck aft of the engine room. They included four berths, several lockers, a lavatory and shower. At the after end of the wheelhouse was a small messroom and galley, with an electric cooker and refrigerator. The forward cabin had stowage for six stretchers and some of the seats could be converted into berths. Attached to it

▼ Deck equipment on 70-001 included an inflatable inshore lifeboat, which was launched by davit. (By courtesy of the RNLI)

CLYDE RESCUE CRUISERS

General Particulars

Operational number	70-001	70-002
Length overall	71ft (21.65m)	70ft (21.4m)
Breadth moulded	18ft (5.49m)	17ft (5.18m)
Depth moulded	10ft (3.05m)	9ft 6in (2.9m)
Fuel capacity	1,189 gallons (5,405 litres)	1,156 gallons (5,255 litres)
Fresh water	210 gallons (955 litres)	230 gallons (1,044 litres)
Load displacement	80.1 tons	78 tons 14 cwt
Load draught, aft	8ft 8in (2.64m)	7ft 8in (2.34m)
Load draught, forward	5ft 7in (1.7m)	5ft 9in (1.76m)
Full speed	11.14 knots	11.2 knots
Endurance (full speed)	560 miles	540 miles
Cruising speed	10.4 knots	10.4 knots
Endurance (cruising speed)	755 miles	730 miles

were a small galley and a lavatory. Abaft of the steering position in the wheelhouse was a chart and radio room. The Clyde was the first RNLI lifeboat with a flying bridge position, which was located atop the main superstructure and had duplicate engine and steering controls.

Two rescue craft were carried: a duty inflatable inshore rescue boat powered by a 33hp outboard motor, which was stowed on the engine casing forward of the wheelhouse and launched by derrick, and a smaller boat of similar type, stowed deflated in the forward cabin, with an 18hp engine. The boats carried over 200 gallons of fresh water, and their electronic equipment included radar, MHF and VHF radios, a Decca navigator, two echo sounders, a loud hailer and an intercom unit linking the various compartments. Standard items of equipment included a searchlight, deck floodlights, breeches buoy, parachute flares, hand flares, scrambling nets, a line-throwing pistol, axes and knives. There were three anchors: standard RNLI pattern anchors in recesses to port and starboard, and a stockless anchor housed in the hawsepipe at the stemhead, which was raised using a hydraulic windlass on the foredeck.

The vessel's hull was divided into six watertight compartments and the engine rooms were separated by a longitudinal centreline watertight bulkhead. Power was provided by twin Gardner 8L3B diesel engines, each developing 230bhp at 1,150rpm. These were the largest and most

powerful engines being built by Gardner at the time. Each engine room also housed a 230-volt A/C generator driven by a 31hp diesel engine, and a 24-volt D/C service was also available. Mathway power-assisted steering gear was used, and in the event of a power failure the steering could be operated manually or by emergency tiller and tackles.

The first Clyde, 70-001, had a maximum speed of 11.14 knots, at which speed she had a range of 560 nautical miles; at her cruising speed of 10.4 knots, with engines at 1,000rpm, the range increased to 755 nautical miles. 70-002 had a top speed of 11.25 knots, at which she had a range of 540 nautical miles; at her cruising speed of 10.4 knots, with engines

▲ 70-002 Grace Paterson Ritchie in London in March 1966. For the visit, she was moored at Tower pier (lower left), with Tower Bridge (top) forming a backdrop. (By courtesy of the RNLI)

CLYDE RESCUE CRUISERS

running at 980rpm, the range was approximately 730 nautical miles; her speed on one engine only was about 9.3 knots.

The £63,907 cost of 70-001 came from the Civil Service Lifeboat Fund, which had provided many lifeboats, and she was initially named Civil Service No.35. Launched in September 1965, she was sailed down the west coast on passage during which she called at Plymouth, Cowes and Dover, before going to London, where she was shown to representatives of the Fund. She was formally named on 4 May 1966, being christened Charles H. Barrett (Civil Service No.35) for the former honorary secretary and treasurer of the Fund, who died on 26 August 1954 at the age of 74. Between 1938 and 1954 Mr Barrett had been the Fund's honorary secretary, assuming the duties of honorary treasurer in 1947. In 1949 the RNLI presented him with a formal Thanks on Vellum for his valuable services, and in 1951 he received the Order of the British Empire.

After her naming, she began a period of sea trials in the form of an extensive tour of the south-west of England, Wales, Ireland and Scotland and in 1966 undertook evaluation trials while based at Clovelly, North Devon, from where she covered St George's Channel, the southern end of the Irish Sea and the mouth of the Bristol Channel. Although

▼ The first 70ft Clyde 70-001 arriving at Plymouth in 1966 during her passage to London, with the nameplate mounted on her after cabin reading RNLB Civil Service No.35. (By courtesy of the RNLI)

◀ The second 70ft Clyde Grace Paterson Ritchie at Ullapool, where she was based during trials in the mid 1960s. (By courtesy of the RNLI)

initially cruising, she operated mainly from moorings at Clovelly, but also sheltered at Lundy Island or on the Welsh side of the Channel at the Mumbles depending on weather and wind direction and strength.

There was concern at the time that silting of the estuaries from where the Appledore and Padstow lifeboats operated had resulted in launching limitations being placed on those stations' lifeboats at low water, and the cruising lifeboat would cover these areas when necessary. After the evaluation trials, it was soon decided to operate the lifeboat mainly from

▼ The second 70ft Clyde Grace Paterson Ritchie on patrol off Scotland.

CLYDE RESCUE CRUISERS

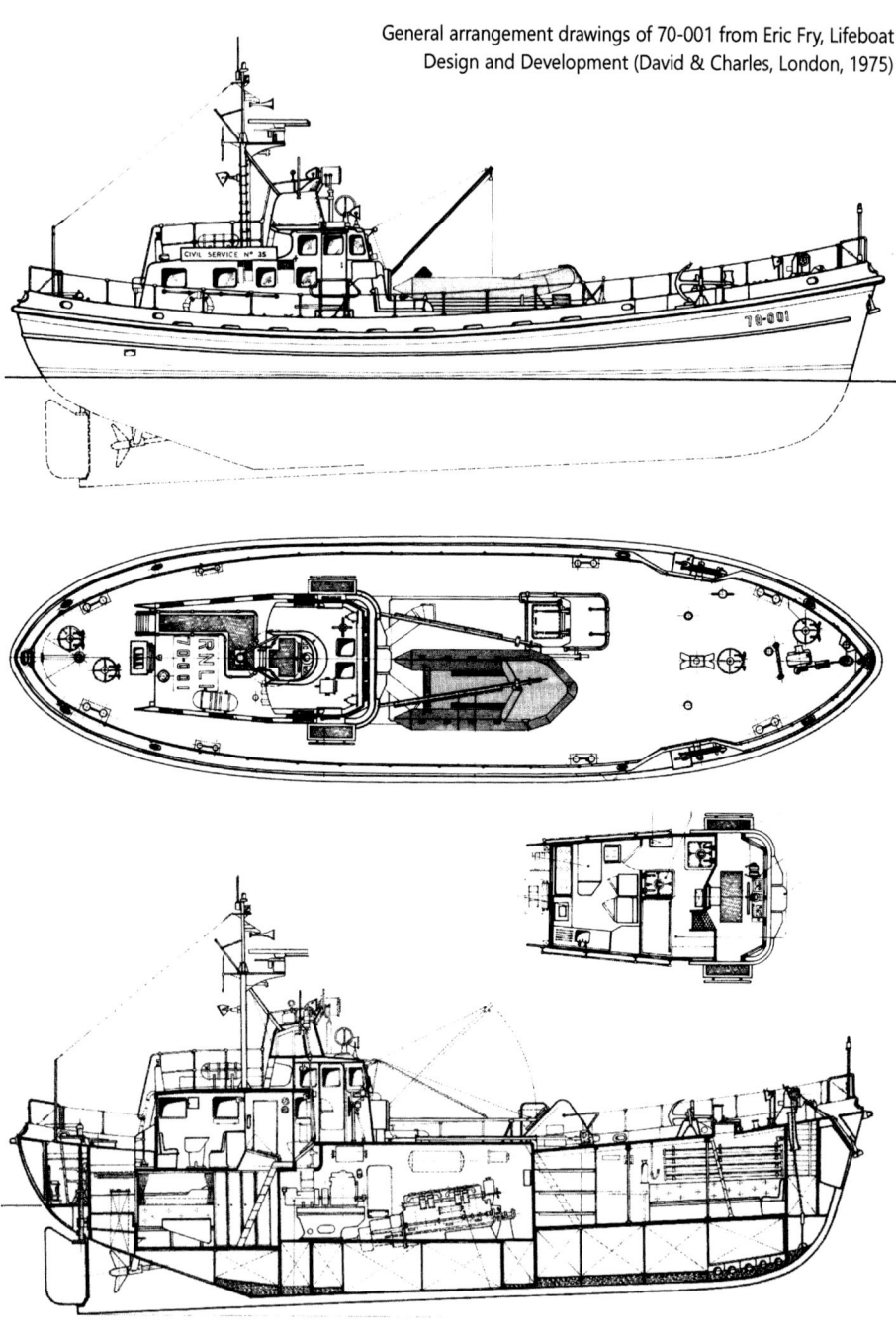

General arrangement drawings of 70-001 from Eric Fry, Lifeboat Design and Development (David & Charles, London, 1975)

▲ The second 70ft Clyde Grace Paterson Ritchie out of the water.

moorings at Clovelly, and as from 31 March 1968 she was known as the Bristol Channel lifeboat. The 35ft 6in Liverpool motor lifeboat William Cantrell Ashley (ON.871), which had been on station at Clovelly since 1949 and was launched over the beach, was withdrawn.

The cost of the second boat, £65,112 19s 9d, was defrayed from a legacy left to the RNLI by Miss Grace Paterson Ritchie, and was named after the donor, whose wish was for the boat to be stationed in Scotland. Following a period of evaluation in the Minch in 1966 and 1967, during which she called at several places during extended trials for the operational assessment to enable RNLI crews to familiarise themselves with this new rescue craft, she was deployed as a cruising lifeboat covering the waters round Orkney and Shetland. She also relieved 70-001 at Clovelly as and when necessary.

The extended trials began as soon as she had been completed by Yarrow Shipbuilders at Greenock, with 70-002 being taken round Scotland and down to London. She went via Troon to Campbeltown, St Kilda to Thurso, Stornoway to Lerwick, Aberdeen to Buckie, Fraserburgh to Peterhead, Aberdeen to Dundee, Leith to River Tyne via the River Tees to Gorleston, and Tower Bridge in London for the capital's flag day on 22 March 1966. After a trip to Southend Pier and back to London with RNLI officials, she left London for further sea trials and evaluation.

These took her to the Channel Islands, where she called at Jersey, Guernsey and Alderney between 24 and 31 March 1966. She then headed to Cowes for an inspection on 13 April 1966. She left the Isle of Wight on passage to Plymouth, then went to Wales, via stops at St Davids to Fishguard, on to Porthdinllaen and Holyhead, then New Brighton to Fleetwood. She crossed to Ireland, visiting Arklow on 24-25 April 1967, Dun Laoghaire on 25-27 April 1967, and Belfast on 27-29 April 1967, ending her tour at Londonderry from 29 April to 1 May 1967. On 2 May 1967 she made the passage across the Northern Channel to Campbeltown and was taken to Yarrow Shipbuilders for survey, arriving

CREWING THE CLYDES • The boats based at Clovelly, 70-001 and then 70-003, were operated by full-time crews, while 70-002 at Kirkwall ended up being crewed mostly by volunteers. Life on board the 70-footers for the full-timers was often challenging with facilities somewhat spartan. The crews consisted of a coxswain, mechanic/engineer and three crew. There was little space, and every crew member had a job to do, taking turns to cook meals and undertake other daily tasks. The crews worked two weeks on, two weeks off, as well as taking annual leave. There were two sets of crew, so each crew member had an opposite number. Everyone had to perform numerous roles when they were on board, and all were trained to use the inflatable boat. In the Bristol Channel, crew changes were usually undertaken at Clovelly, while bunkering was undertaken at Ilfracombe. The boat would also visit Swansea Dock occasionally if, for example, a mechanical problem had to be fixed. Fleet mechanics would usually cover sickness and leave, although crews also covered for each other. The Staff Coxswains had to have deep-sea experience because of the size of the Clydes. Covering the Bristol Channel, the Clydes could be out on service for days. Although this was not usual, during the Fastnet Race in the summer of 1979 70-003 was out searching for many hours in horrendous conditions.

CLYDE RESCUE CRUISERS

▲ The third Clyde rescue cruiser City of Bristol on trials; she was considerably different from the previous two boats of the class.

there at the end of May 1967. After the survey, she was again deployed on cruising operations and performed a duty similar to 70-001 at Clovelly, operating from a base at Kirkwall, in Orkney, covering the treacherous Pentland Firth and the surrounding area.

On 4 March 1968 it was decided to station 70-002 permanently in Orkney's capital, where she became the Kirkwall lifeboat, although she was also available for relief duties at Clovelly if needed. Until 1975 she was commanded by an RNLI inspector or staff coxswain, with a full-time crew. As she was serving as station lifeboat at Kirkwall, by the mid-1970s it was decided she could be operated with just one full-timer, the mechanic, with the rest of the crew being volunteers. This was the case at almost all of the RNLI's other stations.

In the early 1970s the RNLI decided to build a third Clyde class lifeboat. Given the operational number 70-003 (ON.1030), she was initially intended to be a relief for the first two, but ended up serving in the Bristol Channel, leaving 70-001 as the relief vessel. The hull for this third boat was similar to that of 70-001, but the superstructure incorporated modifications based on experience gained in operating the first two Clydes. It was much larger than that on the first two boats, giving the

CLYDE RESCUE CRUISERS

▲ 70-003 (on right) moored alongside 70-001 at Cowes in 1988, when both boats were on the sale list.

boat a completely different appearance, but providing considerably better and more comfortable accommodation for the crews. 70-003 was also completely different internally, had a different deck layout and carried different equipment.

Despite the Clyde cruisers having a long range, and being fully equipped with crew quarters and thus capable of remaining at sea for prolonged periods as completely self-contained units, experience showed this to be an impractical way of maintaining lifeboat cover in UK waters. Even though the boats were placed at locations from where they had relatively large sea areas to cover, working out of operational bases at Clovelly and Kirkwall, cruising operations were not appropriate to the kinds of rescues typically performed by the RNLI's lifeboats. In addition, the Clydes' draught was often too great for many rescue situations, while the boats proved costly to maintain and operate with full-time crews. In the end, the stations at which they were based used them as though they were ordinary lifeboats, and eventually they were replaced by lifeboats of standard designs.

70-001 • Charles H. Barrett

NAME Charles H. Barrett (Civil Service No.35)
DONOR Civil Service Lifeboat Fund.
BUILT 1965, Yarrow & Co, Scotstoun, yard no.2271
OFFICIAL NUMBER 987
COST £63,906 15s 5d
DISPLACEMENT 82 tons
ENGINES Twin 230hp Gardner 8L3B eight-cylinder diesels
STATIONS Trials 2.1966–3.68 (at Ullapool 1966–67), Clovelly 3.1968–9.75 (179 launches/38 saved), Relief 1975–5.1988 (107 launches/58 saved)
DISPOSAL Sold December 1988
RENAMED Poplar Diver/ Dolphin

The naming ceremony of the first Clyde, Charles H. Barrett (Civil Service No.35), took place at St Katharine Docks in London in blustery weather on 4 May 1966. The ceremony was supported by many people, including London schoolchildren and boys of the City of London Sea Scouts. Air Vice-Marshal Sir Geoffrey R. Bromet, KBE, deputy chairman of the RNLI's Committee of Management, opened proceedings by inviting Princess Marina, HRH Duchess of Kent,

▼ RNLB Civil Service No.35 on trials soon after she had been built. (By courtesy of the RNLI)

CLYDE RESCUE CRUISERS

▲ Charles H. Barrett (Civil Service No.35) heads a line-up of rescue craft moored at St Malo for the International Lifeboat Conference in France in 1967. (Grahame Farr, by courtesy of the RNLI)

president of the RNLI, to present a commemorative vellum to the Civil Service Lifeboat Fund to mark the Fund's centenary. The vellum was accepted by Sir Eric A. Seal, chairman of the Fund and a member of the RNLI Committee of Management. The Princess spoke of the 'wonderful example' set by the Fund in raising the money through voluntary donations to pay for the construction of the boat.

Sir Eric responded that the Civil Service Lifeboat Fund was: 'a very remarkable and quite unique body', having started more than a century earlier in the General Post Office and then expanded throughout the Civil Service as a whole. It was established with an annual income of £300, when the average subscription was about six shillings; by the mid-1960s annual income was over £25,000. Sir Eric went on to say: 'The Civil Service Lifeboat Fund decided that the best way to celebrate its centenary is to present the very latest and largest lifeboat ever to the service, and here she is. I will say nothing in praise of her – let her speak for herself'. Air Vice-Marshal Sir Geoffrey Bromet accepted the lifeboat on behalf of the RNLI, and she was dedicated by the Chaplain of the Fleet, the Venerable Archdeacon Christopher Prior. After F.B. Savage, secretary of the Fund, had proposed a vote of thanks, Princess Marina named the lifeboat, and afterwards inspected the lifeboat and spoke to Lt Cdr H.F. Teare and the five crew.

◀ Civil Service No.35 shortly after being completed. (Grahame Farr, by courtesy of the RNLI)

◀ Civil Service No.35 leaving Plymouth in the mid 1960s during her trials. (By courtesy of the RNLI)

◀ Civil Service No.35 undergoing trials on the Clyde in 1966. (By courtesy of the RNLI)

CLYDE RESCUE CRUISERS

▲ Charles H. Barrett (Civil Service No.35) moored by the Cooperative Wholesale Society's depot at Broad Quay in Bristol. (Grahame Farr, by courtesy of the RNLI)

After her naming ceremony, 70-001 was used for almost two years of trials and evaluation to assess her capabilities. On 31 March 1968 she was officially placed on service at Clovelly, and between then and September 1975 when she left Clovelly, Charles H. Barrett (Civil Service No.35) launched 142 times on service and is credited with saving 36 lives. She answered numerous calls each year, performing some fine services, and on two occasions was involved in outstanding rescues.

Outstanding rescues at Clovelly

On 7 November 1971 Charles H. Barrett and her crew undertook a very fine service in particularly challenging conditions. She put out under the command of Staff Coxswain D.J. Reeves to the German motor vessel Embdena, to help a seriously injured man. Dr D. Mackenzie was on board the lifeboat as she sailed to meet Embdena. The wind was south-westerly force eight, with rough seas and a heavy swell. After a passage lasting three and a half hours, against rough seas and a flood tide, the casualty was found at 10pm, twenty-five miles west of Hartland Point, hove-to and rolling and pitching heavily.

Despite the fact that the movements between both vessels was considerable, the lifeboat approached Embdena's starboard side, and, with the assistance of a headrope and engines, Coxswain Reeves brought her alongside the casualty, allowing Dr Mackenzie to jump

across. The dangerous manoeuvre was carried out successfully, and the doctor managed to jump from the lifeboat's rail clear of the ship's bulwark, landing on all fours on her deck, while the lifeboat ranged 15ft alongside. It was then found that the injured man had died. Due to the heavy sea conditions the doctor was not transferred back to the lifeboat until both vessels were in the lee of Lundy Island 20 miles to the north-east. Finally, at 1.30am on 8 November, Dr Mackenzie returned to the lifeboat, which set off for Clovelly, arriving there at 8am. For his bravery in transferring to the casualty vessel, Dr Mackenzie was accorded the Thanks of the Institution inscribed on vellum.

▲ Charles H. Barrett (Civil Service No.35) on trials in the Clyde with invited guests on board to look over the new craft. (By courtesy of the RNLI) ◄

Charles H. Barrett and her crew were again tested in February 1974, facing extreme conditions in the Bristol Channel going to the aid of a fishing vessel. The crew was informed at 2.10am on 6 February that a trawler was sinking 26 miles from Hartland Point and within ten minutes the lifeboat was under way, under the command of Staff

▲ Charles H. Barrett (Civil Service No.35) on a visit to Ilfracombe, 8 July 1966. (Grahame Farr, by courtesy of the RNLI)

Coxswain Michael Houchen. The trawler St Pierre, of Brixham, was taking in water, and its pump was unable to cope. The wind at Clovelly had been westerly force six, but within an hour it had increased to force eight, and conditions became very bad in the Bristol Channel.

Six miles south-west of Lundy, the crew on 70-001 sighted a red flare from St Pierre and altered course towards it. At 5.15am the lifeboat crew reached the trawler, which was heading about north by east and appeared not to be in immediate danger of sinking. By now the wind had reached force 10 to 11, accompanied by violent hail storms, and Staff Coxswain Houchen decided it was too hazardous for St Pierre's crew to be taken on board the lifeboat so he decided to tow the stricken trawler into the lee of Lundy Island.

At 5.40am, with the tow prepared, 70-001 approached St Pierre and Mechanic Ivor Young fired a rocket line. It fell across the trawler, but her crew did not reach it quickly enough and the line slid over the side. Staff Coxswain Houchen approached again, this time on the casualty's lee side, as close as he dare go. Getting the line across was extremely difficult, with seas so heavy that, when both boats were in troughs of the very heavy seas, St Pierre was disappearing from sight of the lifeboat crew. Staff Coxswain Houchen displayed outstanding boat handling

◀ Charles H. Barrett (Civil Service No.35) at her mooring off Clovelly, her regular base in the Bristol Channel, with the steadying sail set. (By courtesy of the RNLI)

skills to get 70-001 within a few feet of St Pierre's quarter after three hazardous approaches. As both boats ranged 20ft and more, Fleet Mechanic Peter Crofts threw the heaving line to the waiting crew on St Pierre and the tow rope was hauled across and secured.

The tow began at 6.20am, making about four knots, and proceeded without incident until 8am, when the vessels entered the Lundy Race. Here the tide was setting against the wind, which was still force 10 to 11, and the result was a phenomenal sea. The waves were about 40ft high, with very steep sides, and at times Staff Coxswain Houchen was standing with his feet on the forward bulkhead of the wheelhouse as he tried to steer 70-001 down the face of a wave. Huge seas stove in the transom of the trawler and one wave broke across the lifeboat and through the top of the wheelhouse door, soaking those inside.

▼ Michael Houchen, one of the Staff Coxswains on 70-001, was awarded the RNLI's Bronze medal for gallantry. (By courtesy of the RNLI)

Houchen later said that, had the tow parted at this point, it would have been the end for the trawler and her crew because he would have been powerless to save them. However, the tow held and the lee of Lundy was reached by about 10am. The lifeboat anchored in Lundy Roads and at 10.30am St Pierre was brought alongside for pumping. By 1.30pm she was about 75 per cent pumped out and it was then discovered that the salvage pump's suction hose was drawing air.

CLYDE RESCUE CRUISERS 25

As the wind had moderated to about force eight, Houchen decided that it would be possible to continue to Ilfracombe with the tow. The anchor was weighed and the tow got under way at 2.20pm, with the vessels arriving at Ilfracombe at about 5pm, where they were secured alongside. While berthed, 70-001 parted two mooring lines, lost a fender and the rubber belting was damaged, so Houchen decided to return to anchor off Lundy once again to shelter from the force eight north-westerly gale, gusting to force nine.

This very challenging service had been completed with the minimum of fuss, and the Clyde lifeboat had proved herself in the most difficult of seas. The Bronze medal for gallantry was awarded to Staff Coxswain Michael Houchen for his leadership and seamanship, and medal service certificates were presented to Mechanics Ivor Young and John Leech, Fleet Mechanic Peter Crofts and Assistant Mechanic Peter Braund.

In September 1975 the new Clyde lifeboat 70-003 replaced 70-001 at Clovelly, and 70-001 was transferred to the Relief Fleet. She spent 13 years as a Relief lifeboat, serving at Kirkwall and Clovelly. After leaving Clovelly she was taken to Mashford's boatyard at Plymouth where she

▼ Charles H. Barrett (Civil Service No.35) in the Bristol Channel with her steadying sail set. (Grahame Farr, by courtesy of the RNLI)

◀ Charles H. Barrett (Civil Service No.35) berthed at Tyne Dock, South Shields towards the end of her career. (By courtesy of the RNLI)

was stored until needed. Her first relief duty was at Clovelly, from March to May 1976, after which she went north for a stint at Kirkwall. The passage between North Devon and Orkney usually took five or six days and she regularly alternated between the two. When not needed at Kirkwall, she would be stored at Herd & Mackenzie's yard at Buckie and between February 1979 and December 1981 she was either at Kirkwall or in Buckie. Her last relief duty at Kirkwall was in early 1987, and her last stint at Clovelly was in March and April 1988, after being stored at Buckie for almost a year, from March 1987 to February 1988.

While in service with the RNLI, 70-001 undertook 290 launches on

◀ Charles H. Barrett (Civil Service No.35) berthed at Poole near the power station in Holes Bay in May 1988 at the end of her RNLI service. (P.W. Tunks)

CLYDE RESCUE CRUISERS

service and saved 101 lives. This included 40 launches and seven lives saved while on passage, 142 launches and 36 lives saved when she was based at Clovelly, 107 launches and 58 lives saved during her period as a relief lifeboat. Between 24 April and 27 May 1988 70-001 was at the RNLI Depot in Poole being prepared for sale. She was moved to the Inshore Lifeboat Centre at Cowes in May, where she remained until being sold out of service in December 1988 for £72,500.

A new owner and a new purpose

70-001 was bought from the RNLI by J.R. Theakston, of Stockton-on-Tees, who took her to Hartlepool. Renamed Poplar Diver, she was altered so that cruising and longer voyages could be undertaken, with sleeping accommodation provided in fore cabins. She was kept at Hartlepool during the winter, and went to Oban in the summer. Theakston usually sailed her to Oban around Easter time. She was used as a dive boat in Scotland, taking up to 12 people on charter trips. By 2000 she had been sold again, and was based permanently on the west coast of Scotland, being kept usually at Kerrera and Tobermory.

▼ Renamed Poplar Diver, 70-001 at Oban in July 1994. (Nicholas Leach)

◀ 70-001 at Hartlepool in January 1989, shortly after being sold out of RNLI service and starting a new chapter in her history. (H.V.J. Cutter)

◀ 70-001, renamed Poplar Diver, anchored off Greenland during her long excursion north in the summer of 1994.

◀ Renamed Poplar Diver, 70-001 at Hartlepool Marina, her home during much of the 1990s.

CLYDE RESCUE CRUISERS

In 2003 she was sold again, as her owner wanted a faster boat. She was bought by Wim van Noortwijk of Hellevoetsluis, a town in the Netherlands, just south of Rotterdam. Wim liked to go to sea when the weather was bad and found his previous boats were not good in rough seas, so wanted 'a boat I can trust'. Renamed Dolphin, she was used mainly for pleasure purposes and cruising around Netherlands

CLYDE RESCUE CRUISERS

▲ Dolphin (70-001) makes a fine sight heading out of Rotterdam, September 2018. (Nicholas Leach)

and further afield. Wim bought her in Oban and, with the previous owner and his son, sailed her through the Caledonian Canal, down the east coast of the UK, and across the North Sea to Maassluis, then to Hellevoetsluis, on a trip that proved her capabilities in all weathers.

The boat was largely original from her service days. However, Wim made changes internally to provide greatly improved accommodation,

ON BOARD DOLPHIN (70-001) AUGUST 2018

Left to right, from the top: the bridge controls; one of the Gardner engines in its engine room; the captain's suite; the galley and saloon; previous owner Wim van Noortwijk (on left) with current owner Gerrit Malipaard on board Dolphin; and twin berths in the forward cabin.

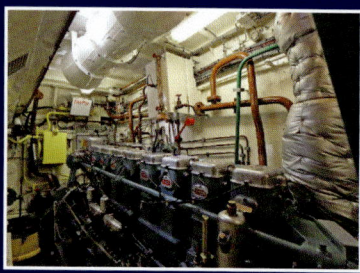

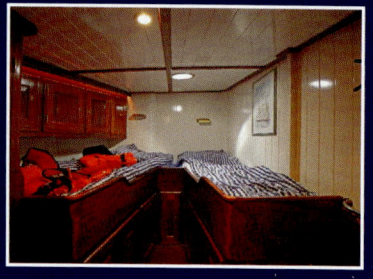

but externally she was left largely as original, apart from the after cabin being extended so that stairs could be installed to improve access to the master cabin. All the electronics were renewed, but the original Gardner engines were in good working order.

Wim used the boat for charter trips, but mainly for pleasure purposes. In 2010 a rowing boat crossing the Atlantic from America to Rotterdam lost its way and Dolphin went out to assist in finding the boat, going as far as the west coast of Ireland, where the boat was located and the four rowers were taken on board. They had not eaten for days and so, as Wim recalled, 'we fed them and brought them back to the route, then escorted them to Rotterdam, over the course of several days'.

In 2016 Gerrit Malipaard, a businessman from Maassluis near Rotterdam, bought the boat from Wim; they were family friends. Gerrit found a permanent mooring for Dolphin in Maassluis, and, her port of registry, Rotterdam on her stern, the boat has cruised extensively under his ownership. She attended Rotterdam World Harbour days in September 2016, and in May 2017 was taken across the North Sea for a visit to Harwich lifeboat station. Many old RNLI crew went on board her while she was in England, and all were keen to look around her and go

▲ Dolphin (70-001) under way off Rotterdam. (Nicholas Leach)

◀ Dolphin (70-001) at Poole to take part in the Lifeboat Festival to mark the 200th anniversary of the RNLI, May 2024. (Nicholas Leach)

▲ Dolphin (70-001) taking part in the Lifeboat Festival at Poole to mark the 200th anniversary of the RNLI, May 2024. (Nicholas Leach)

below decks. She was also taken to Lemmer in September 2016 for the annual gathering of historic lifeboats.

During the winter of 2017-18 the boat was taken out of the water at the shipyard at Maassluis and, over the course of seven months, given a complete refit and extensive refurbishment. All the fixtures and fittings were removed and cleaned, the hull was blasted and repainted, and the engines were dismantled, cleaned and completely rebuilt. The fuel tanks were cleaned and the boat was refurbished throughout. She was in excellent condition when returned to the water in spring 2018, and Gerrit continued to maintain her to a very high standard. She has been refitted to provide eight berths and carries modern navigation equipment.

In 2022 she was cruised to Norway, Bergen and Stavanger, taking in the Norwegian fjords. In May 2024 she crossed the North Sea to Poole, Dorset, to take part in the gathering of modern and historic lifeboats to mark the 200th anniversary of the RNLI. Many former crew members came on board while the boat was at Poole Quay Marina, where she joined other former British and European lifeboats. She took her place in the parade of sail at the culmination of the event, on 19 May, and the following day left the UK to return to her Netherlands home.

70-002 • Grace Paterson Ritchie

NAME Grace Paterson Ritchie
DONOR Legacy of Miss Grace P. Ritchie.
BUILT 1966, Yarrow & Co, Scotstoun, yard no.2272
OFFICIAL NUMBER 988
COST £65,113
DISPLACEMENT 78 tons 14 cwt
ENGINES Twin 230hp Gardner 8L3B eight-cylinder diesels
STATIONS Relief 1966–1975 (54 launches/12 sd)
Kirkwall 3.1968–6.1974 (57 launches/43 saved)
Kirkwall 8.1975–7.1988 (73 launches/29 saved)
DISPOSAL Sold January 1989
RENAMED Henry A. Hálfdánsson/ Grace Ritchie/ Grace Paterson Richie

The second Clyde rescue cruiser was named Grace Paterson Ritchie at a ceremony at Wemyss Bay Pier, on the Firth of Clyde, on 6 September 1967. She was christened by Mrs T. Lyle, a friend of the donor, Miss Grace Paterson Ritchie. Andrew C. Syme, an agent for the trustees of the late Miss Ritchie, handed over the lifeboat to the RNLI on behalf of the trust. Brigadier J.W.H. Gow, a vice president of the RNLI's Committee of Management and chairman of the Glasgow branch, accepted the boat on behalf of the RNLI. The Duke of Atholl, a member of the Committee of Management and Convenor of the Scottish

◀ Grace Paterson Ritchie at sea off Kirkwall. Her naming ceremony at Wemyss Bay in September 1967 was attended by more than 500 people.

CLYDE RESCUE CRUISERS

▲ A fine photograph of Grace Paterson Ritchie off Orkney. During her initial evaluation period, she undertook services all around the country, including at Maplin Sands and Foulness, Lerwick, Loch Rodel, Cape Wrath and Loch Kanaird during 1966. In 1967 she undertook services in the Bristol Channel.

Lifeboat Council, proposed a vote of thanks at the end of the ceremony.

The donor wanted Grace Paterson Ritchie to serve in Scotland and so, after an extensive tour round the coast, she was sent to the north-west of Scotland, being based at Ullapool during the winter of 1966-67 as she carried out operational evaluation trials in The Minch. After the trials, she moved to Orkney to provide cover for the Pentland Firth area. On 4 March 1968 it was decided that she should be based at Kirkwall, but used for relief duties at Clovelly when necessary, so for the winter of 1968-69 she remained at Kirkwall. Before Grace Paterson Ritchie officially became Kirkwall lifeboat, however, as if to confirm that her station would be Orkney's capital, a portable TV set was presented to the boat's crew on 18 December 1967 while she was in port.

As well as Ullapool and Orkney, Grace Paterson Ritchie was operated from various other places. Between 1966 and March 1968 she undertook a number of services from locations, including Lerwick and Loch Broom in Scotland, and Mumbles and Ilfracombe while she was in the Bristol Channel. A testing service took place on 26 October 1966, when she went to the aid of the motor coaster Kathar, which had broken down in gale force winds off Cape Wrath. The lifeboat's services were not needed as, with the trawler Marbella providing assistance, the casualty's crew repaired the engine, but Grace Paterson Ritchie and her crew were out in severe weather for several hours that tested the boat well.

The year 1969 proved to be a particularly difficult one for the lifeboat service. During the night of 17-18 March 1969 the Longhope lifeboat T.G.B., a 47ft Watson, went to the aid of the motor vessel Irene and, in exceptionally severe conditions, was capsized in the Pentland Firth. Tragically, all eight of her crew were drowned. Under the command of Staff Coxswain Ian Cameron Ives, of Whitley Bay, Grace Paterson Ritchie and her crew, from their base at Kirkwall, were tasked to help Irene and, subsequently, T.G.B. They faced appalling conditions in the Firth, and Ives recalled afterwards: 'On that fateful night we encountered the worst seas off Mull Head. We hit one very heavy sea, which was about 60ft high, but the boat behaved beautifully and we have every confidence in her.' Over the whole period of the Longhope tragedy, Grace Paterson Ritchie was at sea for more than sixty hours.

The disaster had a major effect on the local people and the area's rescue services. The Longhope crew, led by Coxswain Dan Kirkpatrick, were part of the tight-knit community on Hoy and everyone on the small island was affected. The loss of T.G.B. meant rescue coverage in the treacherous Pentland Firth area had been significantly reduced, so

▼ Grace Paterson Ritchie in Kirkwall harbour. She served as the Kirkwall lifeboat from 1968 to 1988 following operational trials in the area over the course of several years. (Supplied by Tony Denton)

CLYDE RESCUE CRUISERS

▶ The second 70ft Clyde lifeboat Grace Paterson Ritchie at Kirkwall. (Supplied by Andy Anderson)

▶ Grace Paterson Ritchie in service as the Kirkwall lifeboat. (Supplied by Andy Anderson)

Grace Paterson Ritchie and her Kirkwall crew were tasked to maintain coverage of the Firth while the station at Longhope was re-established, with a new lifeboat being provided and a new crew trained.

She remained at Kirkwall until mid-May 1969, performing a number of routine services, and then left for Bristol, where she was overhauled, returning to Orkney in 1970 and being based in Scapa for much of the summer. In January 1971 she returned to Kirkwall as the Longhope station

◀ Crew members on board Grace Paterson Ritchie in Kirkwall harbour. (Orkney Photographic Archives)

was fully operational again and able to cover the area. Between July and September 1971 she operated from Clovelly, returning to Kirkwall on 16 September 1971. She was then involved in cruising evaluation trials with a full-time crew starting in October 1971. The trials, which lasted until 31 March 1972, took her north of Kirkwall to Orkney's North Isles, where she was based at Stronsay on weekdays and returned to Kirkwall at weekends. But when Kirkwall station was established on 30 May 1972, Grace Paterson Ritchie's role became one of a normal lifeboat crewed mostly by volunteers, and was no longer used for cruising duties in the area.

◀ Grace Paterson Ritchie served at Kirkwall, as the station's first lifeboat, from 1975 until 1988.

CLYDE RESCUE CRUISERS

▲ Grace Paterson Ritchie being led by Charles H. Barrett (Civil Service No.35) in waters off Orkney, with the latter relieving the former.

On 8 November 1971 she was involved in a particularly notable rescue, when four Danish fishing vessels got into difficulty near Kirkwall harbour in deteriorating weather conditions. Two broke adrift and went aground east of Kirkwall pier while the Coastguard attempted to get lines aboard them to prevent them from being further driven ashore. But the Coastguard could not rescue the crews, so, with the northerly wind force ten gusting to hurricane force twelve, the lifeboat put out to help under the command of Staff Coxswain Robin Dennison. The lifeboat managed to tow Rosslau clear of the pier and repeated the operation to get Anne Stranne and the other two stranded vessels, Clupea and Kami, to safety.

Between 8.35am and 1.40pm, Grace Paterson Ritchie and her crew had rescued 20 men and saved four boats, and the lifeboat had proved herself in the worst of weathers. For this excellent service, the Bronze medal was awarded to Staff Coxswain Dennison and Medal Service Certificates went to the remainder of the crew: Dan Grieve, Fred Johnston, Alex Strutt, Jimmy Craigie, Peter Thomson, Mike Drever and Norman Sutherland. The official report stated: 'The action taken by Staff Coxswain Dennison and his crew is to be commended. The highest praise for his seamanship and skill has been voiced by the skippers of the vessels [and] he ensured the safety of 20 lives without loss or injury.'

Between 5 December 1973 and 18 March 1974 Grace Paterson Ritchie was taken to Yarrow Shipbuilders on Clydeside for a routine survey. This was completed on 31 January 1974, after which she was used for further evaluation trials and returned to Kirkwall in spring 1974. In 1975 she visited the Faroe Islands, taking an RNLI delegation to provide advice and information about setting up a rescue service. Leading the delegation was Lt Cdr P.E.C. Pickles, RNVR, RNLI Deputy Chairman, accompanied by Lt Cdr Brian Miles, and Les Vipond, T. Peebles, A. Strutt, J. Ross and S. Poulson. Grace Paterson Ritchie left Buckie on 9 July in thick fog and made for Lerwick. She left Lerwick the following day and then set course for the Faroes. She called at various ports in the Faroes, and returned to Kirkwall after a week, arriving back at her station on 17 July. Before her trip to the Faroes, Grace Paterson Ritchie had been on relief duty at Clovelly from September 1974 to July 1975, but returned to Kirkwall and remained there, with the exception of time away for survey and overhaul, until the late 1980s as the station's lifeboat.

On 22 January 1984 Grace Paterson Ritchie and her crew were involved in another very fine service after the 16-ton fishing vessel Benachie, of Rousay, went ashore on the south of the Island of Rousay, nine miles north of Kirkwall. At 10am, under Coxswain William Sinclair, she headed north at full speed into a force ten wind to help. Very heavy seas were encountered as the lifeboat cleared Shapinsay and the seas became even heavier between the islands of Wyre and Egilsay. At 11.15am, the stranded

◀ Kirkwall lifeboat crew receiving their awards for the rescue on 22 January 1984 of the crew of the fishing boat Benachie. Coxswain Billy Sinclair was awarded the Bronze medal and the remainder of the crew were presented with Medal Service Certificates. The awards were presented by Vice Admiral Sir Peter Compton (on right). The crew are, left to right: Mike Drever, Bobby Hall, Alec Strutt, unknown, Dan Grieve, Billy Sinclair, Geoff Gardens. (Orkney Photographic Archives)

CLYDE RESCUE CRUISERS

▶ Renamed Henry A. Hálfdánsson, 70-002 departs Buckie in March 1989 for Iceland. (By courtesy of Andy Anderson)

▶ Grace Paterson Ritchie in Iceland, renamed Henry A. Hálfdánsson, serving with the Icelandic lifeboat service.

fishing vessel was sighted. Benachie was rolling and the heavy seas were breaking over her, with winds gusting to violent storm force eleven, and snow showers had turned into a blizzard, reducing visibility. Once on scene, Coxswain Sinclair anchored the lifeboat and veered down towards the casualty, with the crew getting a towline across to the vessel, which was pulled clear and escorted to Wyre Pier.

The passage back to Kirkwall was made at reduced speed due to the very rough conditions. For saving three men and their fishing vessel, the Bronze Medal was awarded to Coxswain Captain Sinclair and Medal Service Certificates were presented to Second Coxswain Andrew Grieve,

Mechanic Dupre Strutt, Second Mechanic Robert Mainland, Emergency Mechanics Michael Drever and Michael Foulis, and crew members Robert Hall and Geoffrey Gardens.

Grace Paterson Ritchie left Kirkwall for the last time on 25 July 1988, being replaced by the 52ft Arun Mickie Salvesen. The Clyde was taken to Herd & Mackenzie's boatyard at Buckie, where she was stored prior to being sold out of service. During her career with the RNLI, she launched on service 197 times and is credited with saving 86 lives, as follows: 1966 to March 1968 on passage, Scotland and Bristol Channel, 22 launches; March 1968 to June 1974 at Kirkwall, 82 launches, 46 saved; September 1974 to July 1975, relieving at Clovelly, 20 launches, 11 saved; and from August 1975 to July 1988, at Kirkwall, 73 launches and 29 saved.

She remained at Buckie until being sold out of service for £60,000 on 10 February 1989 to the Lifesaving Association of Iceland. She left Buckie in March 1989 and sailed for Iceland, where she was used as a lifeboat, stationed at Reykjavik. She was renamed Henry A. Hálfdánsson in Iceland after the Icelandic Association's then chairman. The Kirkwall crew kept the boat's bell as a memento of her service in Orkney when she left the station, but decided, when they knew she was continuing to save lives at sea, to return it to the Iceland crew. As Henry A. Hálfdánsson, she served at Reykjavik as a lifeboat for more than a decade, until 2002,

◀ Grace Paterson Ritchie berthed in Largs Marina, May 2005. (Nicholas Leach)

CLYDE RESCUE CRUISERS

▲ Grace Ritchie in the Clyde estuary off Largs, June 2007, under the ownership of Iain Crosbie. (Nicholas Leach)

when she was replaced by a faster lifeboat, which also came from the RNLI. She was then sold by the Icelandic Association, and returned to UK waters under private ownership, renamed Grace Ritchie.

Back in the UK, she was based at Largs Yacht Haven, on the Clyde estuary, and was well maintained under the ownership of Iain Crosbie, being used as a pleasure and diving boat in and around the Clyde estuary and Sound of Bute. Over the weekend of 14-15 July 2007 she was one of several former lifeboats to attend the Clyde River Festival in Glasgow. In November 2013 she was sold, with her new owner also keeping her in Largs. In June 2014 she was at Perth, and was taken to Eyemouth the following year. In November 2018 she changed hands again and was acquired by Bernard Condon, who moved her to Dunstaffnage in March 2019 and the following month to Crinan Boatyard for work to her hull. She was then taken to Coleraine in May 2019, having been formally renamed Grace Paterson Ritchie. Bernard was also the owner of the 47ft Watson lifeboat Joseph Soar (Civil Service No.34) (ex-ON.971) and the two former lifeboats were usually moored together on the River Bann.

With the boat in Coleraine, Bernard began a logistically challenging

◀ Grace Ritchie heading up the River Clyde to Glasgow for the Clyde River Festival, July 2007. (Nicholas Leach)

◀ Grace Ritchie in Glasgow in July 2007 for the Clyde River Festival, during which she was moored in front of Crown Plaza Hotel. (Nicholas Leach)

CLYDE RESCUE CRUISERS

▶ Grace Ritchie at Eyemouth in September 2015. (Cliff Crone)

▼ Grace Paterson Ritchie out of the water during the restoration work.

▼ (right) Owner Bernard Condon in the wheelhouse of Grace Paterson Richie. He said: "The honour of receiving the 2024 Martyn Heighton Award is somewhat overwhelming. Martyn's volumes have been our go-to for years, and we never in our wildest dreams imagined we'd be worthy of his name".

restoration over the course of four years, including having to face the restrictions of Covid lockdowns. Bernard and his colleagues Pippin McGrath and Ishabel MacIntyre stopped counting after they had put in well over 26,000 hours of work on the boat. Bernard's mission with 70-002 is to use her to promote and preserve the RNLI's heritage and contribute to its future. She is used exclusively in promotion and fundraising for present and future RNLI generations. Bernard's considerable efforts were recognised in November 2024 when National Historic Ships UK presented him with the 2024 Martyn Heighton Award for Excellence in Maritime Conservation for his exemplary conservation of the boat, having returned her to in-service condition with ninety-five per cent of the original hull and fittings intact. The NHS-UK Judging Panel were particularly pleased to award the trophy to Bernard as he was the first private owner to win the Award since it was launched in 2019.

▲ Grace Paterson Ritchie on the River Bann at Coleraine, Northern Ireland, September 2024.

◀ On board Grace Paterson Ritchie.

▼ The inside accommodation on Grace Paterson Ritchie is much as it was when she was in RNLI service, with galley and wheelhouse largely unaltered.

CLYDE RESCUE CRUISERS

70-003 • City of Bristol

NAME City of Bristol
DONOR Special Appeal in Bristol, together with legacies from Mrs Q. Rimer, Dr S.M. Riddick, S.V. Shrosbree and H. J. Vagg.
BUILT 1974, Bideford Ship Yard, North Devon, yard no.Y44
DIMENSIONS 71ft x 18ft
OFFICIAL NUMBER 1030

COST £196,000
DISPLACEMENT 87 tons
ENGINES Twin 230hp Gardner 8L3B eight-cylinder diesels
STATIONS Clovelly 9.1975–8.1988 (191/84)
DISPOSAL Sold December 1988
RENAMED John V. Story/ Gemini Storm/ Gemini Explorer

The third and last Clyde, 70-003, was built initially as a relief vessel for the other two, but ended up being placed in operational service at Clovelly. She had a hull similar to that of the first boat, but modifications to the superstructure and layout below decks, based on experience gained from operating the first two vessels, were incorporated. She was thus significantly different in many respects from the first two Clydes, although she was fitted with the same engines: twin

▶ The third Clyde class lifeboat, City of Bristol, on trials; she was built in North Devon at Bideford Shipyard, one of only a handful of lifeboats to be completed by this yard. (By courtesy of the RNLI)

CLYDE RESCUE CRUISERS

Gardner 8L3B diesels, each developing 230bhp at 1,150rpm. These gave her a cruising speed of ten knots; she had a radius of action at full speed of 350 nautical miles and could remain at sea for several days.

The hull was divided longitudinally by five watertight bulkheads, and the space below the tank top was subdivided into watertight compartments. The boat carried equipment similar to that on the earlier boats, including two inflatable rescue boats. One was kept inflated on the

◄ City of Bristol was very different in appearance from the earlier Clyde boats; she had a displacement of 87 tons, she was larger than the two earlier boats. She had accommodation for her crew of five below decks. (By courtesy of the RNLI)

◄ City of Bristol at William Osbrone's boatyard, Littlehampton, 2 July 1974. (Jeff Morris)

CLYDE RESCUE CRUISERS 49

◤ City of Bristol arriving in Bristol for her naming ceremony in 1974. (By courtesy of the RNLI)

aft deck, with a 33hp outboard engine; the other was stowed deflated in the forward cabin, with its 18hp engine. Crew accommodation was provided below deck forward in a cabin with three berths, lockers, a toilet and shower. Separate cabins were provided aft for the coxswain and mechanic. A galley and messroom were forward of the wheelhouse.

Named City of Bristol, 70-003 was built at Bideford Shipyard in North Devon. She was completed during the summer of 1974 and undertook a series of extensive visits. Between 19 July and 17 August she was a popular exhibit at the Lifeboat International Exhibition at Plymouth, held to mark the 150th anniversary of the RNLI. She joined several other lifeboats for the event, which was attended by thousands of visitors. She remained in Plymouth for most of August 1974, and on 30 August went from the south coast port to Bristol, commanded by Staff Coxswain Captain Roy Harding, for her naming ceremony.

During the ceremony, held at Narrow Quay in St Augustine's Reach, Bristol on Sunday 1 September 1974, 70-003 was named City of Bristol by the Lady Mayoress of Bristol, Mrs Peglar. The Lord Mayor of Bristol, Councillor A.G. Peglar, announced the launching of the Bristol lifeboat appeal to raise £150,000 within a year, to offset the cost of the new lifeboat. As well as the Bristol appeal, funding for the boat came from

◀ City of Bristol at Bristol for her naming ceremony on 1 September 1974. (By courtesy of Jeff Morris) ▼

CLYDE RESCUE CRUISERS

▶ The Lady Mayoress of Bristol, Mrs A.G. Peglar, with Captain Roy Harding (on left) and crew members, at the naming of City of Bristol. (By courtesy of the RNLI)

▼ City of Bristol was christened at Bristol on 1 September 1974 and stayed in the city for a week. She is pictured passing Pill on 9 September, with Shirehampton in the background, as she departed Bristol. (Grahame Farr, by courtesy of the RNLI)

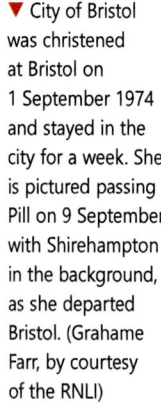

the legacies of Mrs Rimer, Dr Riddick, Mr Vagg and Mrs Shrosbee.

City of Bristol was placed on station at Clovelly on 12 September 1975, replacing 70-001, and spent almost 13 years at the North Devon station. She was taken away for overhaul at various times, usually going to Mashford's yard at Plymouth for the work to be undertaken, although on one occasion, in early 1984, she went to Holyhead Boatyard. In June 1977 she took part in the Silver Jubilee Fleet Review at Spithead when HM The Queen, aboard HMY Britannia, reviewed the Fleet as part of celebrations marking her Silver Jubilee. The Clyde was one of three

◀ City of Bristol at Plymouth for the RNLI's 150th anniversary celebrations during the summer of 1974. Rescue craft of various sizes from Germany, France, Norway, Poland and Sweden took part in the events at Plymouth, along with five RNLI lifeboats.

lifeboats taking part, and was under the command of Tom Nutman, Divisional Inspector (Scotland, North).

During her time at Clovelly, City of Bristol launched 193 times on service and is credited with saving 84 lives, undertaking a number of challenging rescues. On 13 December 1978, while she was on service to the French fishing vessel Alcyon, she was 'knocked down' by a huge wave in the severe conditions, but came back upright. Although a 'no service' assessment was made of the incident by the RNLI, the lifeboat and her crew were at sea for many hours in heavy weather.

City of Bristol undertook a very fine service on 9 January 1981. She put out from Clovelly at 10.18pm, under the command of Staff Coxswain Roger Smith, to stand by the chemical tanker Pass of Dirriemore, which suffered engine failure between Hartland Point and Lundy Island. There were 12 people on board. It was a squally night with a force eight gale gusting to severe gale force nine, and rough seas. When City of Bristol reached Pass of Dirriemore the tanker was five miles west of Hartland and a tug from Milford Haven was requested.

By 12.45am on 10 January the tanker was about six miles south-west of Hartland Point, and was being driven towards the coast. At 2am her anchor was let go, with the wind having risen to severe gale force nine. City of Bristol continued to stand by until, at 6am, the tug Glen Garth arrived on scene. The lifeboat crew helped pass a tow between tug and

◀ City of Bristol at Spithead in June 1977, with 52ft Arun Joy and John Wade, which was completing her trials before going on station at Yarmouth, Isle of Wight. The boats were two of three lifeboats present for the Fleet Review to mark HM The Queen's Silver Jubilee. (By courtesy of the RNLI)

tanker, which was attached by 8am. Pass of Dirriemore then weighed anchor and Glen Garth began the tow to Milford Haven so the lifeboat was released. While she had been standing by the tanker, City of Bristol experienced some electrical and mechanical troubles.

Assistant Fleet Mechanic Tony Dixon, with the help of another crew member, tried to make the necessary repairs at sea, in the very difficult conditions. As the gale had not moderated, this proved impossible so it was decided to make for Swansea Bay, where City of Bristol anchored in Port Talbot Roads to complete her repairs at 4.30pm. For this service, a

◀ City of Bristol in Ilfracombe harbour at low water. While based at Clovelly, she would often call in at the North Devon harbour.

▲ City of Bristol at her mooring off Clovelly, August 1984. (Tony Denton)

◀ City of Bristol off Clovelly. (By courtesy of the RNLI)

letter of appreciation signed by Rear Admiral W. J. Graham, director of the RNLI, was sent to Staff Coxswain Roger Smith and his crew.

At 9.29pm on 11 July 1987 City of Bristol, under the command of Staff Coxswain Roger Smith, was launched to the aid of the 29ft yacht Moon Dragon, which was in need of immediate assistance two miles west of Hartland Point. A Wessex helicopter from RAF Chivenor arrived at the casualty first and airlifted a five-year-old girl to safety. The pilot decided that further lifts would be unsafe because of the yacht's violent motion, as she was lying with her beam to the seas. The lifeboat arrived at

10.07pm, and Helmsman Robert Carswell and crew member Laurence Conibear took the inflatable rescue boat to the casualty, bringing the woman and two more children safely to City of Bristol. The survivors, suffering from seasickness, were taken below to be made comfortable.

The D class inflatable then returned for the casualty, with Helmsman Carswell and crew members Conibear and Michael Bowden on board, and Bowden was transferred onto the yacht, after which the inflatable was hoisted back aboard 70-003. Bowden helmed the yacht clear of the race, then headed north before turning for Clovelly, with the lifeboat following. On arrival at Clovelly, the three survivors were landed ashore to a waiting ambulance. The lifeboat escorted the yacht to moorings at Clovelly, and was back at her moorings at 1.25am after a four-hour service. For this rescue, a framed letter of thanks, signed by RNLI chairman, the Duke of Atholl, was sent to Coxswain Smith, Mechanic John Spillane and crew members Bowden, Conibear and Carswell.

During the mid-1980s, as the RNLI continued with its policy of building faster lifeboats, the Clyde cruisers had become outdated and, in August 1988, 70-003 was withdrawn from Clovelly and the station was closed. She had spent her entire service career in the Bristol Channel area and left Clovelly for the last time on 15 August 1988, arriving at the RNLI Depot at Poole two days later. For the remainder of 1988 she was kept at the power station berth in Poole and then moved to Cowes on the sale list. On 1 December 1988 she was sold out of service to the Kent and Essex Sea Fisheries Committee, County Hall, Maidstone, Kent for £140,000 to be used as a fisheries protection vessel in the south-east of England, and

▲ The deck layout of City of Bristol, pictured during the 1980s just before she was sold out of service, with the inflatable removed, along with various other pieces of equipment. ▶

◀ City of Bristol arriving at Plymouth in August 1988 for an overnight stay during her final journey from Clovelly following the closure of the station. She was on her way to the RNLI Depot at Poole. (Ann Parsons)

◀ 70-003 at Ramsgate, renamed John V. Story, working for Kent & Essex Sea Fisheries. (Nicholas Leach)

◀ 70-003 renamed John V. Story and on patrol in the Thames Estuary, working for Kent & Essex Sea Fisheries. (Nicholas Leach)

was renamed John V. Story after the organisation's chairman.

Based at Ramsgate, she spent more than ten years patrolling the Thames Estuary, until, in about 2000, she was sold again. Bought by a Scottish owner, she was taken to Buckie Shipyard where, during the summer of 2000, she was surveyed. She was part-owned by the owner of 70-001, and joined 70-001 as a diving boat on the west coast. Renamed Gemini Storm, she was operated mainly out of Oban, but often visited other harbours, including Fort William and Tobermory.

In 2001-02 she had an extensive refit at Buckie Shipyard, with three additional cabins, a new galley and a reconfiguration of the saloon area, providing a total of 16 berths, comprising two double and 12 single berths. She changed hands again in 2003 and in 2004 returned to Buckie shipyard for more extensive work, which reportedly cost £500,000; her bulwarks were raised forward, and rear wings and an after deck were constructed to provide a large deck area above the saloon for observing sea life. She was based at Buckie and, renamed Gemini Explorer, was used as a wildlife and dolphin watch boat. In 2017 she was offered for sale for £195,000. She changed hands during 2018 and in September 2018 was sailed from Buckie through the Caledonian Canal to the Clyde, becoming a charter boat based at Dunstaffnage Marina, Oban in 2019.

▼ 70-003 at Buckie Shipyard in August 2000, prior to being extensively converted. (Nicholas Leach)

◀ 70-003 at Buckie, renamed Gemini Explorer, taking out a party of wildlife watchers, July 2014. (Cliff Crone)

▼ On board Gemini Explorer during a wildlife watching trip, July 2014. (Cliff Crone)

◀ 70-003, renamed Gemini Explorer, heads west on the Caledonian Canal, passing through Inverness in September 2018. (Alasdair MacLean)

CLYDE RESCUE CRUISERS

Map

Map showing the places where the Clyde rescue cruisers served, visited or were based after service. The principal stations served were Clovelly, in the Bristol Channel, and Kirkwall, the Orkney capital.

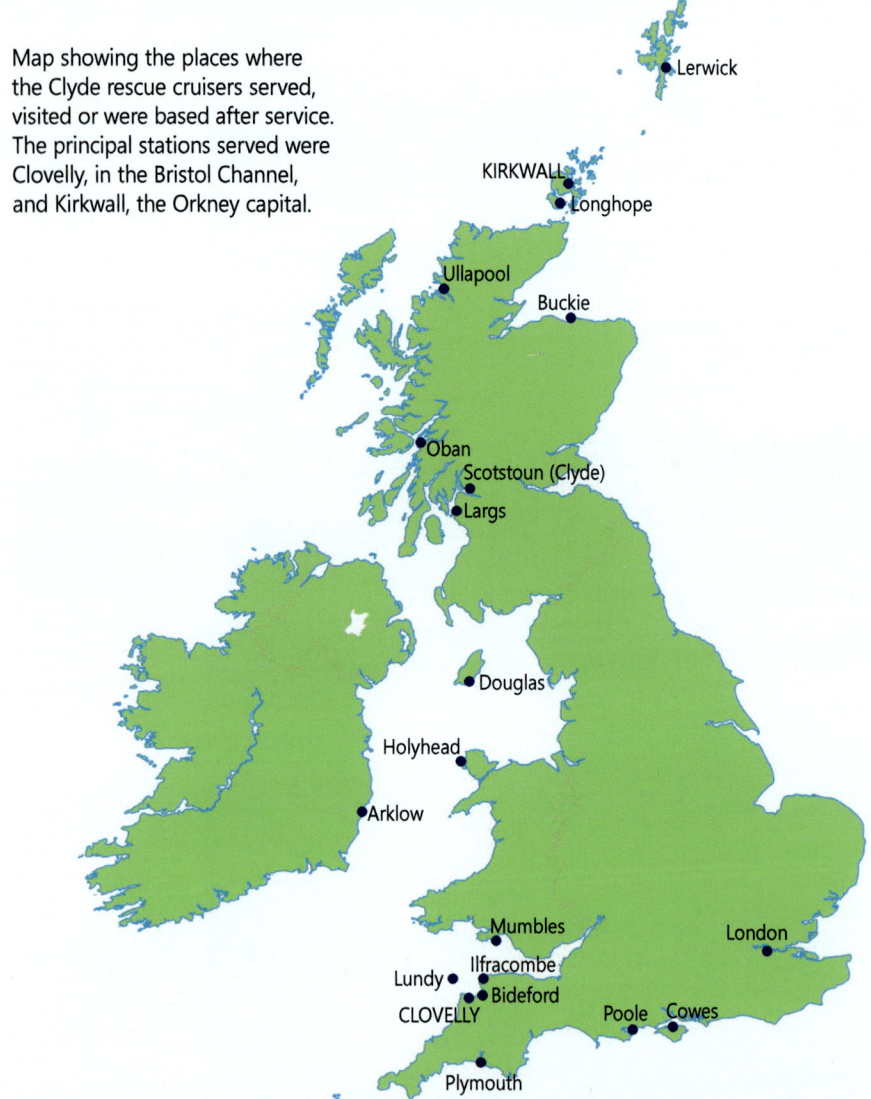